ON THE
ROAD TO
REVOLUTION

BY ANN ROSSI

PEARSON
Scott
Foresman

Editorial Offices: Glenview, Illinois • Parsippany, New Jersey • New York, New York

Sales Offices: Needham, Massachusetts • Duluth, Georgia • Glenview, Illinois
Coppell, Texas • Ontario, California • Mesa, Arizona

Setting the Scene: The American Colonies in 1763

From 1756 to 1763, all the great powers of Europe were engaged in the Seven Years' War. France, Austria, Great Britain, Russia, and many other countries battled over land in Europe—and over their colonies. The part of this war that was fought in North America came to be known in the United States as the French and Indian War.

When the Seven Years' War ended in 1763, and the French and Indian War with it, Great Britain had won most of France's North American territories. Great Britain was now one of the most powerful countries in the world, and many American colonists were pleased to be part of this powerful empire. However, tensions between Great Britain and its colonies would soon develop.

With the war over, King George III of Great Britain began to take an active interest in his now much larger colonies in the Americas. Unfortunately for King George, new ideas were becoming popular in the 1700s — ideas that would make it difficult for him to control his colonies.

The term "natural rights" was beginning to be used in political debates and in writing. People began discussing the rights of the individual. Among the many rights they discussed were the rights to be free, to own property, and to participate in government.

People in the Thirteen Colonies had come to enjoy rights and freedoms that people in Europe only discussed. When new laws were passed, many colonists felt that the British government was interfering with their rights and freedoms.

This map shows the thirteen American colonies in 1763.

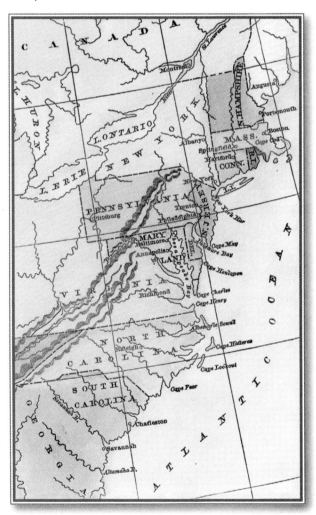

Sowing the Seeds of Conflict

The Seven Years' War had left Great Britain with huge debts, so some of the growing interest in the colonies was interest in colonial money. Many British leaders felt that Britain's American colonies should help pay the war debts. After all, were the colonists not loyal subjects of the king? Had they not benefited from having the French defeated?

In 1764 the British government enacted the first in a series of tax laws that they hoped would increase **revenues**, or money coming in, from the American colonies. The Revenue Act of 1764, also called the Sugar Act, set taxes on sugar and molasses from non-British ports. In addition to raising revenue, this act was designed to stop colonists from buying sugar from French and Dutch traders. The taxes angered many colonists, who wanted to buy less expensive sugar, even if they were buying from Great Britain's enemies.

The following year, the British passed the Stamp Act, which required colonists to pay a tax on documents, newspapers, and other materials printed in the colonies. The colonists were outraged, and many refused to pay.

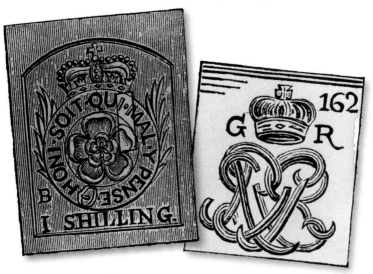

Tax stamps such as these could be attached to printed materials to show that the tax had been paid.

Representatives from nine colonies met in New York to protest the Stamp Act. They pointed out that colonists were British subjects, and that one of their rights was that only their elected representatives could tax them. Because they had no representatives in Parliament, the colonists argued, Parliament should not tax them. They accused Parliament of **tyranny**, the cruel or unfair use of power. The slogan "Taxation without representation is tyranny" became popular.

Colonists were not buying British goods, which hurt British merchants. Also, Parliament realized that it was unlikely that it would ever collect much revenue from this tax, so the Stamp Act was **repealed** in 1766.

The same year in which the Stamp Act was passed, 1765, Parliament passed the Quartering Act. This law required colonists to care for British soldiers stationed in the American colonies. British lawmakers felt that colonists should help pay for the soldiers who were protecting the colonies. Colonists were responsible for providing food, drink, housing, coal or firewood, and candles to troops stationed in their towns.

Many colonists obeyed the Quartering Act, but because many resented it, they often provided fewer supplies than the soldiers needed. The colony of New York had to support the largest number of soldiers, so tensions were greatest there. When the New York Assembly refused at first to assist with quartering British troops, a fight occurred, and a colonist was wounded.

At the same time Parliament repealed the Stamp Act, in 1766, it issued the Declaratory Act. This act stated that Parliament had the right to tax the colonies for any reason. It was not until the next year that colonists learned what would be taxed next.

In 1767 Britain passed the Townshend Acts. One of these laws prohibited the New York Assembly from conducting business until it met the requirements of the Quartering Act. Another law created **tariffs** on many imported goods. A third

British soldiers arrive at Long Wharf, Boston Harbor, 1768.

act established a system of customs, or tax collection, in the colonies and included a Board of Customs Commissioners in Boston. In 1768 soldiers were sent to Boston to keep order and to enforce the Townshend Acts.

Angry colonists organized **boycotts** of British goods, which hurt British merchants. On March 5, 1770, the British Parliament agreed to repeal some of the taxes. However, it did not repeal the tax on tea. That same day, an incident occurred in Boston that would dramatically increase anti-British feelings in the colonies.

Violence Erupts

Fistfights between soldiers and colonists were becoming fairly common in Boston. On March 5, 1770, however, a much more serious incident occurred. According to some reports, a threatening crowd had surrounded a group of British soldiers outside the Custom House. The crowd rapidly grew in size, taunting the soldiers and hurling objects at them. The commanding officer told his soldiers to hold their fire. However, when a snowball hit a soldier, first one startled soldier and then another fired into the crowd. In the end, three people were killed, and eight more were wounded. Two of the wounded later died.

This picture by Paul Revere is not really accurate, but it shows how the people of Boston felt about the shootings, and it helped fuel anti-British feelings.

John Adams

A Patriot leader who opposed Britain's right to tax the American colonies, John Adams still upheld the rights of the British soldiers involved in the Boston Massacre. His defense of the soldiers made him unpopular for a time, but Adams continued to be an important Patriot leader. He was elected to the First Continental Congress in 1774. In 1797 he became the second President of the United States.

Patriots, or colonists who opposed British rule, called the incident the Boston Massacre. Newspaper accounts picked up the name, and soon many colonists were rallying in opposition to British policies in the colonies. Although the killing of five people could not be defined accurately as a **massacre**—the needless killing of a large number of people—it was a violent event that showed how strained relations between the colonists and the British had become.

Like many colonists, Samuel Adams thought the use of soldiers against civilians was a symbol of tyranny. He proclaimed that the Boston Massacre was a battle for American liberty.

The British soldiers were put on trial. Lawyer John Adams, a cousin of Samuel Adams, and his assistant, Josiah Quincy, defended them. Adams argued that the crowd had provoked the soldiers, and therefore the soldiers were innocent of murder. Two of the soldiers were later found guilty of manslaughter, which meant they hadn't planned to kill anyone. As was the custom in those days, the two guilty of manslaughter were branded on their thumbs as punishment.

After the Boston Massacre

The British withdrew their troops to an island in Boston Harbor shortly after the Boston Massacre, thanks in part to the efforts of Samuel Adams. In 1772 Adams and other Boston leaders formed a Committee of Correspondence. Express riders delivered their correspondence, or letters, to other communities, keeping them informed of local events and how groups of Patriots hoped to stop Great Britain's interference. This network of writers and riders helped unite the colonies.

Tea and the East India Company

The East India Company, formed in 1600, imported spices and cloth from India. In the 1700s, it began importing tea from China. Tea became very popular in Great Britain—more popular than drinks that were taxed. So tea was taxed. The British were as unhappy as the colonists would be later. Tea smuggling became common, which hurt the East India Company. However, the company was a source of revenue for the British government, so the government created laws to protect it. One law stated that tea could be sold in the colonies only by agents of the East India Company. This looked to the colonists as though the government was controlling the tea trade. It was this, even more than the tax, that caused the colonists to rebel against the Tea Act.

This picture shows Patriots destroying tea during the Boston Tea Party.

Samuel Adams also organized resistance to the Tea Act. The tax on tea still existed after the Townshend Acts had been repealed in 1770. After all, the British government needed to have some way of showing that it had the right to tax the colonies. However, the colonists had gotten around this tax by buying tea smuggled in by Dutch traders.

In 1773 the British passed the Tea Act, a law that reduced taxes on tea and made it easier for the East India Company to sell tea to the colonies. It also stated that only agents of the East India Company could sell the tea to stores in the colonies. So independent shippers and traders in the colonies were going to lose business.

The tea in this bottle was collected by T.M. Harris, Dorchester Neck, December 1773.

The East India Company's tea would be able to compete with the smuggled tea because their prices would be the lowest available, even though the tea was still taxed! But the colonists did not like the idea of the British government taxing them, and despite the lower price, they would not buy the tea.

Although tea was much loved in the colonies, merchants in New York, Philadelphia, Charleston, and other cities canceled tea orders or refused shipments. However, the British-appointed governor in Boston wanted to obey the law. He insisted that three ships waiting in the harbor be allowed to unload their cargo of tea—and that they be paid for it.

A group of Patriots had other plans for the tea. On the night of December 16, 1773, a group of about sixty men disguised themselves as Mohawks and boarded the ships. A larger crowd of Bostonians had come with them, and they watched from the docks as the smaller group dumped chest after chest of tea into the harbor. Colonists knew this was an important event, and some collected samples of tea as souvenirs.

Heading Toward Revolution

Parliament passed several laws in 1774 to punish Bostonians and to show others what could happen if they defied British authority. Colonists called these the Intolerable Acts, because they were **intolerable**, or unbearable. The port of Boston was closed, unapproved town meetings were banned, and British soldiers returned. Samuel Adams sent letters throughout the colonies pointing out that Britain could interfere with other colonial governments, just as it had in Massachusetts.

From September 5 to October 26, 1774, representatives from every colony except Georgia gathered in Philadelphia for the First Continental Congress. They voted to cease trade with Britain until the Intolerable Acts were repealed. Most of the representatives were not in favor of independence, but they agreed to begin strengthening their **militias**. They also agreed to a second meeting in May 1775 if Britain had not changed its policies by then.

In February 1775 Britain declared that Massachusetts was in open rebellion. Two months later, General Gage, who now controlled Boston, received secret orders to arrest leaders of the rebellion, including Samuel Adams. The Patriot leaders learned of this and fled to Lexington.

Samuel Adams

On April 18, 1775, Patriots in Boston learned that British soldiers were planning a nighttime march to Lexington, to search for the Patriot leaders, and then to Concord, to destroy Patriot supplies. They knew that the militia must be warned!

At 11 P.M., Paul Revere galloped on horseback out of Boston to warn militias and leaders that the British were coming. William Dawes and Samuel Prescott joined him along the way. The three reached Lexington, but a British patrol stopped them as they left. Only Prescott escaped to reach Concord. However, the militia had been alerted by Prescott, and **minutemen** were ready when the British arrived in Lexington.

The next day, fighting began between British soldiers and American Patriots in Lexington, Massachusetts. No one knows who fired the first shot, but it marked the beginning of the Revolutionary War in America.

Key Events on the Road to Revolution

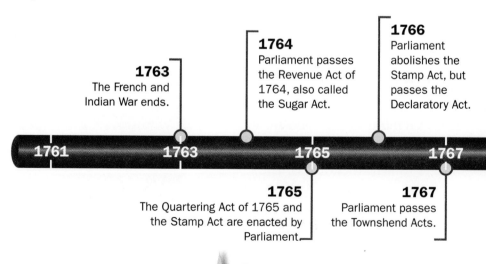

1763
The French and Indian War ends.

1764
Parliament passes the Revenue Act of 1764, also called the Sugar Act.

1766
Parliament abolishes the Stamp Act, but passes the Declaratory Act.

1761   1763   1765   1767

1765
The Quartering Act of 1765 and the Stamp Act are enacted by Parliament.

1767
Parliament passes the Townshend Acts.

14

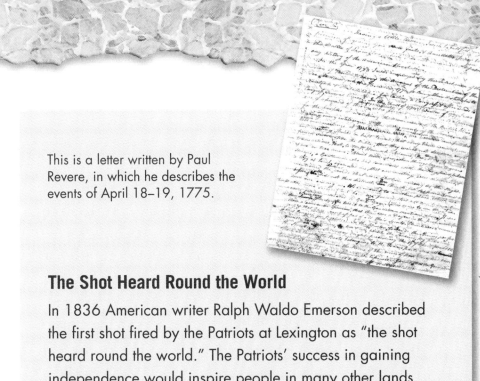

This is a letter written by Paul Revere, in which he describes the events of April 18–19, 1775.

The Shot Heard Round the World

In 1836 American writer Ralph Waldo Emerson described the first shot fired by the Patriots at Lexington as "the shot heard round the world." The Patriots' success in gaining independence would inspire people in many other lands to fight for the independence of their own countries.

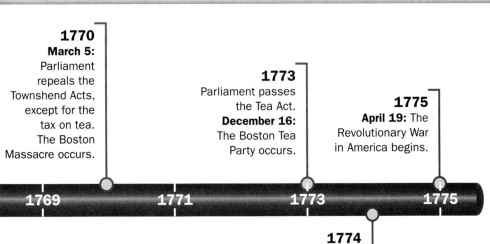

1770
March 5: Parliament repeals the Townshend Acts, except for the tax on tea. The Boston Massacre occurs.

1773
Parliament passes the Tea Act.
December 16: The Boston Tea Party occurs.

1775
April 19: The Revolutionary War in America begins.

1769 — 1771 — 1773 — 1775

1774
Parliament passes the Intolerable Acts.
September 5–October 26: The first Continental Congress meets in Philadelphia.

Glossary

boycott organized refusal to buy goods

intolerable unbearable; too much to be endured

massacre the cruel and needless killing of many people

militia a volunteer army

minutemen colonial militia groups that could be ready to fight at a minute's notice

Patriot a colonist who opposed British rule of the American Colonies

repeal to cancel

revenue money coming in; income

tariff a tax on imported goods

tyranny cruel or unfair use of power